SCHOLASTIC ★ EXPLAINS™

MATH HOMEWORK

SCHOLASTIC
REFERENCE

Produced by Kirchoff/Wohlberg, Inc.
Editorial Director, Mary Jane Martin

CREDITS

Design and Electronic Production: Kirchoff/Wohlberg, Inc.

Illustration: John Wallner, 4, 5, 12, 13, 14, 15; Liz Callen, 8, 9, 22, 23, 53; Eileen Hine, 10, 34, 40, 56, 57; Tom Leonard, 16, 17, 33, 35, 36, 37, 38, 39, 40, 41, 51, 57, 60; Andy San Diego, 18, 19, 20, 42, 43; Rosekrans Hoffman, 24, 25, 26, 27; Diane Paterson, 29, 55; Brian Cody, 30, 31; Jared Lee, 44; Nicole Rutten, 45; Diane Blasius, 59, 61; Andrea Wallace, 62.

Photo Acknowledgments: 3, Lawrence Migdale/Tony Stone Images; 7, Jerry Jacka Photography; 9, Comstock; 16, John Gajda/FPG International; 17, Laura Dwight/PhotoEdit; 26, HP Merten/ The Stock Market; 32, Stephen Simpson/FPG International; 36, Robert E. Daemmrich/Tony Stone Images; 37, Doug Armand/Tony Stone Images; 38, Ian Murphy/Tony Stone Images; 39, Mark Joseph/Tony Stone Images; 40, Roy Morsch/The Stock Market; 41, Mugshots/The Stock Market; 43, Tom McCarthy/Third Coast Stock Source; 48, Leo De Wys, Inc.; 50, Edward McCormick/The Stock Market; 52, Aaron Rezny/The Stock Market; 54, PhotoDisc; 58, Flip Chalfont/The Image Bank; 58-63 (BACKGROUND), Phototone.

Board of Advisors

Library of Congress Cataloging-in-Publication Data

Scholastic Explains math homework: everything children (and parents) need to survive 2nd and 3rd grade.
p. cm. (The Scholastic Explains homework series)

Summary: Explains the facts and procedures of basic math concepts likely to be found in homework.
ISBN 0-590-39754-0 (hardcover)   ISBN 0-590-39757-5 (pbk.)

1. Mathematics—Study and teaching (Elementary)—Juvenile literature.
[1. Mathematics.]   I. Scholastic Inc.   II. Title: Math homework   III. Series
QA135.5.S295   1998   97-38782   513-dc21   CIP   AC

Table of  Contents

A Note to Parents

Your child is hard at work on math homework. Everything seems fine. But then comes that moan of frustration. This kid needs help.

You may not have had to think about some of these math topics for a good many years. You may find some new and unfamiliar terms included in the homework. The homework instructions may be difficult to understand, incompletely copied, or just plain missing. That's where this book comes in.

When you first bring this book home, browse through the table of contents with your child. Ask your child which topics seem familiar. Knowing what your child knows will help you to help your child with homework problems.

When you want to find a particular topic, look it up in the index. You may find the subject using the term your child uses (*regrouping*, for example) or the term you remember (*carrying*). Either way will lead you to the right pages. Then just work with your child, reading the explanation and sharing the examples.

At right is a guide to two typical pages from *Scholastic Explains Math Homework*, with the elements you will find throughout the book.

That's all there is to it. Happy homework!

---

explanation in language used in the classroom

homework subject

easy-to-follow directions

Addition

ADDING 2-DIGIT NUMBERS
without regrouping

When you add 2-digit numbers, first add the ones place. Then add the tens place.

	Tens	Ones
You have	3	2
Add	+ 2	4
		6

ADDING ONES

Tens   Ones

Start with the ones place.
2 ones and 4 ones are 6 ones.
Write 6 in the ones place.

	Tens	Ones
You have	3	2
Add	+ 2	4
	5	6

ADDING TENS

Tens   Ones

Add the tens.
3 tens and 2 tens are 5 tens.
Write 5 in the tens place.
The sum of 32 and 24 is 56.

THESE PLACE-VALUE BLOCKS HELP YOU SEE TENS AND ONES.

THE ANSWER IN ADDITION IS THE SUM OR TOTAL.

The plus sign means add.

$32 + 24 = 56$

THIS MEANS EQUAL.

NUMBERS YOU ADD ARE CALLED ADDENDS.

12

examples for doing homework assignment

Index

new subject

helpful hints

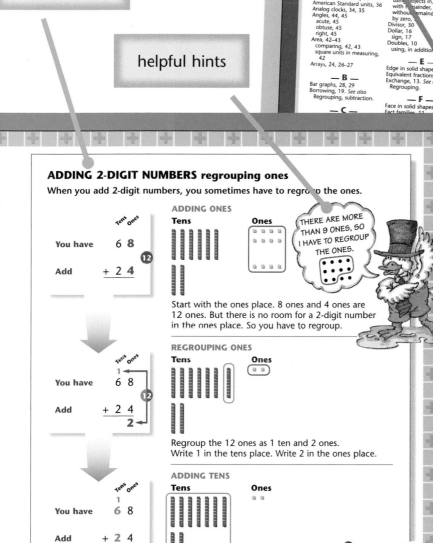

ADDING 2-DIGIT NUMBERS regrouping ones

When you add 2-digit numbers, you sometimes have to regroup the ones.

ADDING ONES

THERE ARE MORE THAN 9 ONES, SO I HAVE TO REGROUP THE ONES.

Start with the ones place. 8 ones and 4 ones are 12 ones. But there is no room for a 2-digit number in the ones place. So you have to regroup.

REGROUPING ONES

Regroup the 12 ones as 1 ten and 2 ones.
Write 1 in the tens place. Write 2 in the ones place.

ADDING TENS

Add the tens. Add the 1 ten you regrouped to the 6 tens and 2 tens. The sum is 9 tens.
The sum of 68 and 24 is 92.

NOTE
Words that also mean regroup are **exchange**, **trade in**, and **carry**.

13

find topics in ABC order at the end of the book, on page 64

other words used by teachers

models and illustrations children recognize

Again and Again

PATTERNS

A **pattern** is an order of things repeated over and over.

These jelly beans are not in a specific order.
They are not in a pattern.

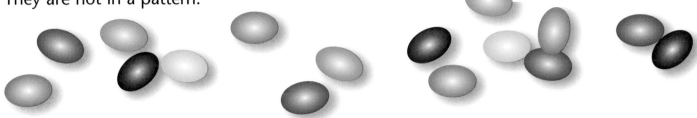

These jelly beans are in specific orders that repeat.
They are in patterns.

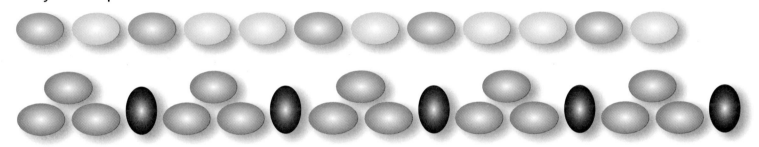

This pattern repeats red circle and red square.
This is an AB pattern.

This pattern repeats blue circle and red square.
This is also an AB pattern.

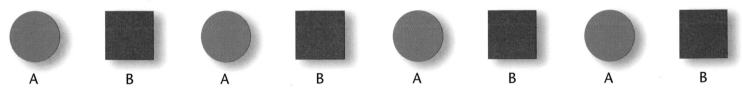

Here is an ABC pattern.

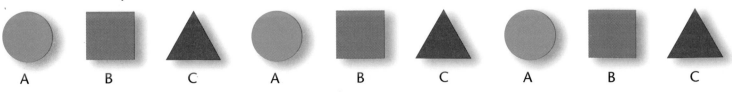

These are Native American blankets with repeated pattern shapes and colors. The weavers are using an AAA pattern.

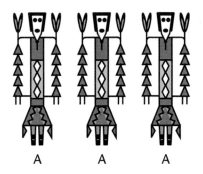

A   A   A

 NOTE

Once you recognize and describe a pattern, you can tell how to continue the pattern.

These patterns have many shapes and colors.

This is an ABBCC pattern.

A   B   B   C   C   A   B   B   C   C   A   B   B   C   C

This is an ABBCD pattern.

A   B   B   C   D   A   B   B   C   D   A   B   B   C   D

This is an ABB pattern.

A   B   B   A   B   B   A   B   B   A   B   B

This is an ABC pattern.

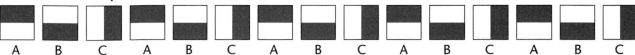

A   B   C   A   B   C   A   B   C   A   B   C   A   B   C

The Right Place

PLACE VALUE hundreds, tens, and ones

You use only ten digits to write numbers. Here they are!

0 1 2 3 4 5 6 7 8 9

Place value in any number shows the meaning of each digit. When you do your homework, be sure you know the value of each digit you write. The digit's place in the number tells how many it stands for.

The value of a digit changes when the place of a digit changes. Zero holds the place when there aren't any other digits for that place.

2

Here the digit 2 means 2 ones.

That's how many eggs the hen has.

20

Here the digit 2 means 2 tens.

There are 0 ones. She has 20 eggs now.

200

Here the digit 2 means 2 hundreds.

There are 0 tens and 0 ones. Wow! 200 eggs!

You can use place-value blocks to show numbers.

These blocks show 323.

3 hundreds   2 tens   3 ones

These blocks show 204.

2 hundreds   0 tens   4 ones

This is called a place-value chart.

This chart shows **145**.

hundreds	tens	ones
1	4	5

1 hundred   4 tens   5 ones
100   40   5

MAKE A CHART WHEN YOU DO YOUR HOMEWORK.

When you work with large numbers, it will help you to make a place-value chart.

This chart shows **64,537**.

ten thousands	thousands	hundreds	tens	ones
6	4	5	3	7

6 ten thousands   4 thousands   5 hundreds   3 tens   7 ones
60,000   4,000   500   30   7

PUT A COMMA BETWEEN HUNDREDS PLACE AND THOUSANDS PLACE.

In the number 64,537
- the 6 is in the ten thousands place, so the 6 means 60,000.
- the 4 is in the thousands place, so the 4 means 4,000.
- the 5 is in the hundreds place, so the 5 means 500.
- the 3 is in the tens place, so the 3 means 30.
- the 7 is in the ones place, so the 7 means 7.

NOTE

Here are three ways to write the same number:
Standard form: 64,537
Expanded form:
60,000 + 4,000 + 500 + 30 + 7
Words:
sixty-four thousand, five hundred thirty-seven

Addition and Subtraction

HELPFUL HINTS

Using a Number Line

Add on a number line. Start at the first number and **count on**.

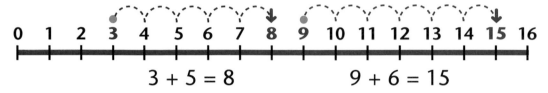

$$3 + 5 = 8 \qquad\qquad 9 + 6 = 15$$

Subtract on a number line. Start at the first number and **count back**.

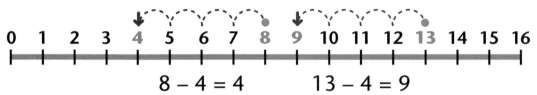

$$8 - 4 = 4 \qquad\qquad 13 - 4 = 9$$

Using Doubles

When you add, doubles can help you.

If you know $5 + 5 = 10$,
then you know $5 + 6 = 11$.

THE SUM MUST BE 1 MORE THAN 10 BECAUSE 6 IS 1 MORE THAN 5.

Using Zero

When you add or subtract, knowing about 0 can help you.

If you add 0 to any number, the sum is that number.

$$7 + 0 = 7 \qquad\qquad 4 + 0 = 4$$

If you subtract 0 from any number, the difference is that number.

$$5 - 0 = 5 \qquad\qquad 8 - 0 = 8$$

If you subtract a number from itself, the difference is 0.

$$9 - 9 = 0 \qquad\qquad 6 - 6 = 0$$

Comparing Numbers

Use these signs to compare sets of numbers.

This sign < means is less than.
$$4 < 9$$

This sign > means is greater than.
$$9 > 4$$

The arrow always points to the smaller number.

Using Fact Families

When you change the order of the numbers you add (called the addends), the sum is the same.

$3 + 4 = 7$ $4 + 3 = 7$

Every addition fact has one or more related subtraction facts.

$3 + 4 = 7$ so $7 - 4 = 3$

A fact family is a group of related addition and subtraction facts. Here is a fact family:

$4 + 3 = 7$ $3 + 4 = 7$ $7 - 3 = 4$ $7 - 4 = 3$

ADDITION FACTS TABLE

0 + 0 0	0 + 1 1	0 + 2 2	0 + 3 3	0 + 4 4	0 + 5 5	0 + 6 6	0 + 7 7	0 + 8 8	0 + 9 9
1 + 0 1	1 + 1 2	1 + 2 3	1 + 3 4	1 + 4 5	1 + 5 6	1 + 6 7	1 + 7 8	1 + 8 9	1 + 9 10
2 + 0 2	2 + 1 3	2 + 2 4	2 + 3 5	2 + 4 6	2 + 5 7	2 + 6 8	2 + 7 9	2 + 8 10	2 + 9 11
3 + 0 3	3 + 1 4	3 + 2 5	3 + 3 6	3 + 4 7	3 + 5 8	3 + 6 9	3 + 7 10	3 + 8 11	3 + 9 12
4 + 0 4	4 + 1 5	4 + 2 6	4 + 3 7	4 + 4 8	4 + 5 9	4 + 6 10	4 + 7 11	4 + 8 12	4 + 9 13
5 + 0 5	5 + 1 6	5 + 2 7	5 + 3 8	5 + 4 9	5 + 5 10	5 + 6 11	5 + 7 12	5 + 8 13	5 + 9 14
6 + 0 6	6 + 1 7	6 + 2 8	6 + 3 9	6 + 4 10	6 + 5 11	6 + 6 12	6 + 7 13	6 + 8 14	6 + 9 15
7 + 0 7	7 + 1 8	7 + 2 9	7 + 3 10	7 + 4 11	7 + 5 12	7 + 6 13	7 + 7 14	7 + 8 15	7 + 9 16
8 + 0 8	8 + 1 9	8 + 2 10	8 + 3 11	8 + 4 12	8 + 5 13	8 + 6 14	8 + 7 15	8 + 8 16	8 + 9 17
9 + 0 9	9 + 1 10	9 + 2 11	9 + 3 12	9 + 4 13	9 + 5 14	9 + 6 15	9 + 7 16	9 + 8 17	9 + 9 18

Addition

ADDING 2-DIGIT NUMBERS
without regrouping

When you add 2-digit numbers, first add the ones place. Then add the tens place.

	Tens	Ones
You have	3	**2**
Add	+ 2	**4**
		6

ADDING ONES

Tens | **Ones**

Start with the ones place.
2 ones and 4 ones are 6 ones.
Write 6 in the ones place.

THESE PLACE-VALUE BLOCKS HELP YOU SEE TENS AND ONES.

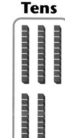

	Tens	Ones
You have	**3**	2
Add	+ **2**	4
	5	**6**

ADDING TENS

Tens | **Ones**

Add the tens.
3 tens and 2 tens are 5 tens.
Write 5 in the tens place.

The sum of **32** and **24** is **56**.

THE ANSWER IN ADDITION IS THE SUM OR TOTAL.

The plus sign means add.

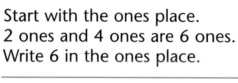

$$32 + 24 = 56$$

NUMBERS YOU ADD ARE CALLED ADDENDS.

THIS MEANS EQUAL.

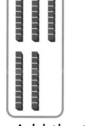

ADDING 2-DIGIT NUMBERS regrouping ones

When you add 2-digit numbers, you sometimes have to regroup the ones.

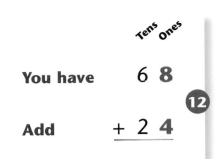

You have   **6 8**

Add   **+ 2 4**

12

ADDING ONES

Tens   **Ones**

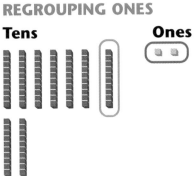

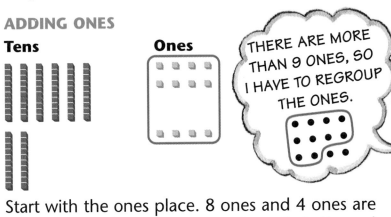

THERE ARE MORE THAN 9 ONES, SO I HAVE TO REGROUP THE ONES.

Start with the ones place. 8 ones and 4 ones are 12 ones. But there is no room for a 2-digit number in the ones place. So you have to regroup.

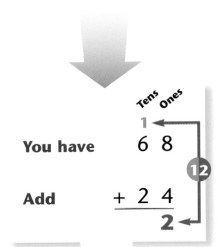

You have   **6 8**

Add   **+ 2 4**

2

12

REGROUPING ONES

Tens   **Ones**

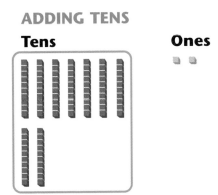

Regroup the 12 ones as 1 ten and 2 ones.
Write 1 in the tens place. Write 2 in the ones place.

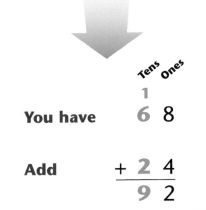

You have   **6** 8

Add   **+ 2 4**

9 2

ADDING TENS

Tens   **Ones**

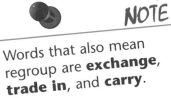

Add the tens. Add the 1 ten you regrouped to the 6 tens and 2 tens. The sum is 9 tens.

The sum of 68 and 24 is 92.

NOTE

Words that also mean regroup are **exchange**, **trade in**, and **carry**.

ADDING 3-DIGIT NUMBERS
regrouping ones

When you add 3-digit numbers, you sometimes have to regroup.

THESE PLACE-VALUE BLOCKS HELP YOU SEE HUNDREDS.

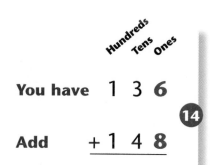

	Hundreds	Tens	Ones
You have	1	3	**6**
Add	+ 1	4	**8**

14

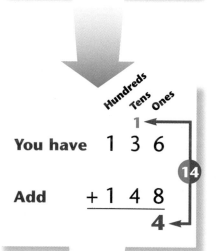

		Hundreds	Tens	Ones
			1	
You have		1	3	6
Add		+ 1	4	8
				4

14

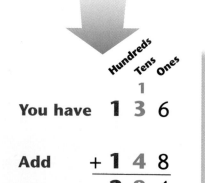

	Hundreds	Tens	Ones
		1	
You have	**1**	3	6
Add	+ **1**	4	8
	2	**8**	4

ADDING ONES

Hundreds **Tens** **Ones**

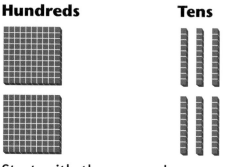

Start with the ones place.
6 ones and 8 ones are 14 ones.

REGROUPING ONES

Hundreds **Tens** **Ones**

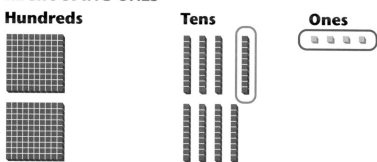

Regroup the 14 ones as 1 ten and 4 ones.
Write 1 in the tens place.
Write 4 in the ones place.

ADDING TENS AND HUNDREDS

Hundreds **Tens** **Ones**

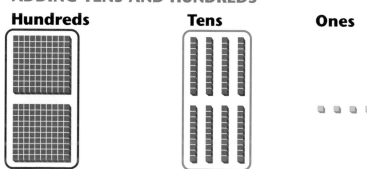

Add the tens. Then add the hundreds.
The sum of 136 and 148 is 284.

ADDING 3-DIGIT NUMBERS
regrouping tens

THE NUMBER 271 HAS 3 DIGITS. THE 2 IS A DIGIT. SO IS THE 7 AND 1.

Here's another way to show 3-digit addition:

You have **2 7 1**

Add **+ 1 5 3**

4

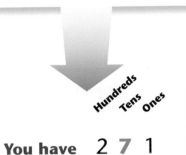

You have **2 7 1**

Add **+ 1 5 3**

4

⑫

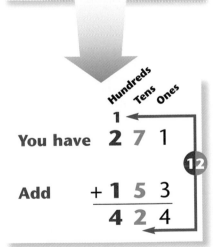

1

You have **2 7 1**

Add **+ 1 5 3**

4 2 4

⑫

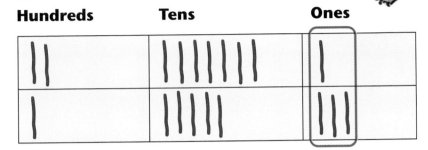

ADDING ONES

Hundreds	Tens	Ones

Start with the ones place.
1 one and 3 ones are 4 ones.

ADDING TENS

Hundreds	Tens	Ones

Add the tens.
7 tens and 5 tens are 12 tens.

REGROUPING TENS, ADDING TENS AND HUNDREDS

Hundreds	Tens	Ones

12 tens is the same as 1 hundred and 2 tens.
Regroup the 12 tens as 1 hundred and 2 tens.
Write 1 in the hundreds place.
Write 2 in the tens place.
Then add the hundreds.
The sum of 271 and 153 is 424.

Counting Coins

SKIP COUNTING

Here are five types of United States coins:

penny

1¢ or $.01
one cent

nickel

5¢ or $.05
five cents

dime

10¢ or $.10
ten cents

quarter

25¢ or $.25
twenty-five cents

half dollar

50¢ or $.50
fifty cents

When you count money, skip count coins that are alike.

To skip count nickels, count by 5s.

5¢	10¢	15¢

15 cents

To skip count dimes, count by 10s.

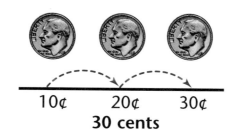

10¢	20¢	30¢

30 cents

To skip count quarters, count by 25s.

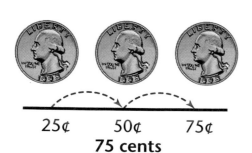

25¢	50¢	75¢

75 cents

To skip count half dollars, count by 50s.

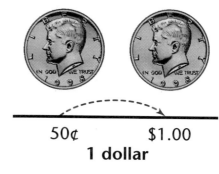

50¢	$1.00

1 dollar

COUNTING ON

When you count coins that are different, it is helpful to **count on**.

Count on like this:

25¢   35¢   36¢

25 and 10 is 35 and 1 is 36

Before you count this group of coins, arrange them from greatest to least value.

Then count on.

	(+25¢)	(+10¢)	(+5¢)	(+1¢)

50¢ ⟶ 75¢ ⟶ 85¢ ⟶ 90¢ ⟶ 91¢

You can show the same amount of money using different coins. Here are three ways to make 32 cents:

25¢ ⟶ 30¢ ⟶ 31¢ ⟶ 32¢

10¢ ⟶ 20¢ ⟶ 30¢ ⟶ 31¢ ⟶ 32¢

10¢ ⟶ 20¢ ⟶ 25¢ ⟶ 30¢ ⟶ 31¢ ⟶ 32¢

NOTE

A **decimal point** is used with a dollar sign. When you use the cent sign, do not use a decimal point.
$.35 = 35¢, NOT .35¢

17

Subtraction

SUBTRACTING 2-DIGIT NUMBERS
without regrouping

When you subtract 2-digit numbers, first subtract in the ones place. Then subtract in the tens place.

	Tens	Ones
You have	9	7
Subtract	− 4	5
		2

	Tens	Ones
You have	9	7
Subtract	− 4	5
	5	2

SUBTRACTING ONES

Tens

Ones

XXXXX

Start with 7 ones.
Subtract 5 ones.
There are 2 ones left.
Write 2 in the ones place.

SUBTRACTING TENS

Tens

Ones

Start with 9 tens.
Subtract 4 tens.
There are 5 tens left.
Write 5 in the tens place.

The difference between 97 and 45 is 52.

THE X OVER A PLACE-VALUE BLOCK SHOWS THAT BLOCK WAS SUBTRACTED.

THE ANSWER IN SUBTRACTION IS THE DIFFERENCE OR THE REMAINDER.

THE NUMBER YOU SUBTRACT FROM IS THE MINUEND.

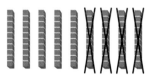

The minus sign means subtract.

97 − 45 = 52

THE NUMBER YOU SUBTRACT IS THE SUBTRAHEND.

SUBTRACTING 2 DIGIT NUMBERS with regrouping

When you subtract 2-digit numbers,
you sometimes have to regroup the tens.

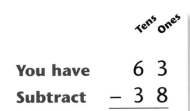

	Tens	Ones
You have	6	3
Subtract	− 3	8

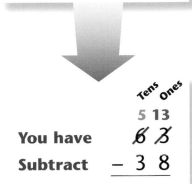

SUBTRACTING ONES

Tens	Ones

Start with the ones place. Subtract 8 ones.
You can't subtract 8 ones from 3 ones,
so you need to regroup to get more ones.

REGROUPING TENS

Tens	Ones
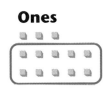	

Regroup 1 ten as 10 ones. Instead of 3 ones,
you have 13 ones. Cross out 3 and write 13 in
the ones place. Instead of 6 tens, you have 5
tens. Cross out 6 and write 5 in the tens place.

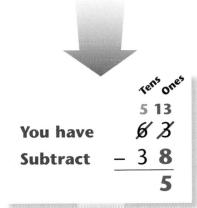

SUBTRACTING ONES

Tens	Ones
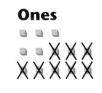	

Now you can subtract the ones.
13 ones minus 8 ones equals 5 ones.

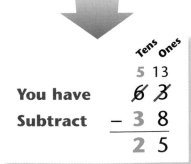

SUBTRACTING TENS

Tens	Ones

Subtract the tens. 5 tens minus 3 tens equals 2 tens.
The difference between 63 and 38 is 25.

SUBTRACTING 3-DIGIT NUMBERS
regrouping tens

When you subtract 3-digit numbers, first subtract in the ones place. Next subtract the tens. Then subtract the hundreds place.

REMEMBER TO KEEP EACH DIGIT IN THE RIGHT PLACE.

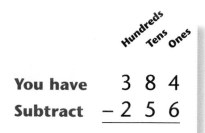

You have 3 8 4
Subtract − 2 5 6

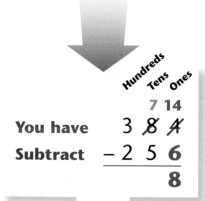

7 14
You have 3 8̸ 4̸
Subtract − 2 5 6
          8

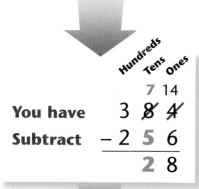

7 14
You have 3 8̸ 4̸
Subtract − 2 5 6
        2 8

7 14
You have 3 8̸ 4̸
Subtract − 2 5 6
      1 2 8

SUBTRACTING ONES

Hundreds	Tens	Ones

Start with the ones place. Subtract 6 ones from 4 ones. You can't subtract 6 ones from 4 ones, so you need to regroup to get more ones.

REGROUPING TENS AND SUBTRACTING ONES

Hundreds	Tens	Ones

Regroup 1 ten as 10 ones. Instead of 4 ones, you have 14 ones. Write 14 in the ones place instead of 4. Instead of 8 tens, you have 7 tens. Write 7 in the tens place instead of 8. Now you can subtract the ones.

SUBTRACTING TENS

Hundreds	Tens	Ones

Subtract the tens.

SUBTRACTING HUNDREDS

Hundreds	Tens	Ones

Subtract the hundreds.
The difference between 384 and 256 is 128.

SUBTRACTING 3-DIGIT NUMBERS regrouping hundreds

Here's another example of subtracting with 3-digit numbers.
This shows how to regroup hundreds.

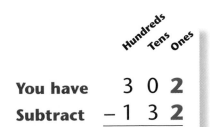

SUBTRACTING ONES

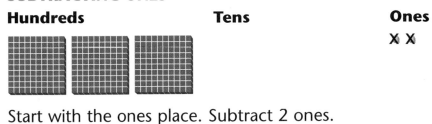

Start with the ones place. Subtract 2 ones.

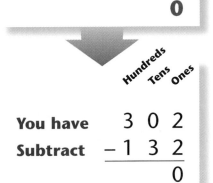

SUBTRACTING TENS

Hundreds | Tens | Ones

Subtract the tens.
You can't take 3 tens from 0 tens,
so you need to regroup to get more tens.

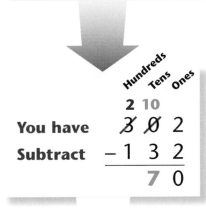

REGROUPING HUNDREDS AND SUBTRACTING TENS

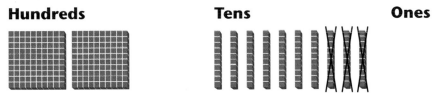

1 hundred is the same as 10 tens, so regroup
1 hundred as 10 tens. Instead of 0 tens, you have
10 tens. Write 10 in the tens place. Instead of 3
hundreds, you have 2 hundreds. Write 2 in the
hundreds place instead of 3. Now subtract the tens.

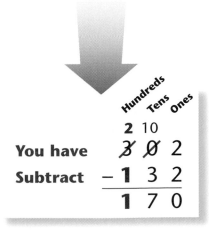

SUBTRACTING HUNDREDS

Subtract the hundreds.
The difference between 302 and 132 is 170.

Round Up!

ROUNDING NUMBERS

When you estimate you need to **round** a number to the nearest ten.

You can use a number line to help you find the nearest ten. Here's how to round 13 to the nearest ten:

0 1 2 3 4 5 6 7 8 9 10 11 12 **13** 14 15 16 17 18 19 **20** 21

1. Find the tens that 13 is between: 10 and 20.
2. Decide if 13 is closer to 10 or to 20.
3. See that 13 is closer to 10, so 13 rounds down to 10.

Here's how to round 27 to the nearest ten:

15 16 17 18 19 **20** 21 22 23 24 25 26 **27** 28 29 **30** 31 32

1. Find the tens that 27 is between: 20 and 30.
2. Decide if 27 is closer to 20 or to 30.
3. See that 27 is closer to 30, so 27 rounds up to 30.

Things to Remember When Rounding a Number to the Nearest Ten

If the number in the ones place is 1, 2, 3, or 4, round **down** to the nearest ten.

Round down 2**2** to 20.   Round down 4**4** to 40.

If the number in the ones place is 5, 6, 7, 8, or 9, round **up** to the nearest ten.

Round up 5**8** to 60.   Round up 6**9** to 70.

NOTE

Some people always round a number ending with 5 up. Some people round up or down.

Sometimes you will need to round a number to the nearest hundred.

Here's how to round 140 to the nearest hundred:

100 110 120 130 **140** 150 160 170 180 190 200 210 220

1. Find the hundreds that 140 is between: 100 and 200.
2. Decide if 140 is closer to 100 or to 200.
3. See that 140 is closer to 100, so 140 rounds down to 100.

Here's how to round 270 to the nearest hundred:

200 210 220 230 240 250 260 **270** 280 290 300 310

1. Find the hundreds that 270 is between: 200 and 300.
2. Decide if 270 is closer to 200 or to 300.
3. See that 270 is closer to 300, so 270 rounds up to 300.

THAT'S OK TOO.

WHEN THE NUMBER ENDS WITH 50, I ROUND UP OR DOWN.

Things to Remember When Rounding a Number to the Nearest Hundred

If the number in the tens place is 0, 1, 2, 3, or 4, round **down** to the nearest hundred.

Round down 6**3**0 to 600.   Round down 5**0**1 to 500.

If the number in the tens place is 5, 6, 7, 8, or 9, round **up** to the nearest hundred.

Round up 5**7**9 to 600.   Round up 3**8**1 to 400.

Multiplication

A FAST WAY TO ADD

When you **multiply**, you put together groups to find out how many there are in all.

6 × 7 = 42

THE NUMBERS YOU MULTIPLY ARE FACTORS.

The sign × means multiply. You say "times."

$$\begin{array}{r} 7 \\ \times 6 \\ \hline 42 \end{array}$$

THE ANSWER IN MULTIPLICATION IS THE PRODUCT.

Using Repeated Addition
Since multiplication is repeated addition, you can figure out an answer by adding.

3 × 4 is the same as 4 + 4 + 4.
The sum of 4 + 4 + 4 is 12.
The product of 3 × 4 is 12.

Using Objects
You can model multiplication with groups of objects.

For 3 × 4, show 3 groups of 4. Then count the cubes.

This shows 3 × 4 = 12.

Using an Array
This array has 3 rows of 4.

When you count, you can see that 3 × 4 = 12.

 NOTE

An **array** is an arrangement of columns and rows that stands for two factors. The total number of units in the array shows the product.

Using a Number Line
You can skip count on a number line to show multiplication.

For 3 × 4, start at 0. Skip count by 4s, three times. You end on 12.

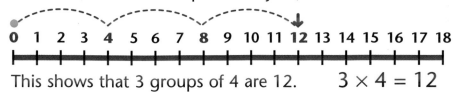

This shows that 3 groups of 4 are 12.   3 × 4 = 12

MULTIPLICATION FACTS TABLE

It's important to know multiplication facts. You can use a multiplication facts table like this to find the product of any multiplication from 0×0 to 9×9. The red numbers are factors. The black numbers are products.

↓ columns

×	0	1	2	3	4	5	6	7	8	9
0	0	0	0	0	0	0	0	0	0	0
1	0	1	2	3	4	5	6	7	8	9
2	0	2	4	6	8	10	12	14	16	18
3	0	3	6	9	12	15	18	21	24	27
4	0	4	8	12	16	20	24	28	32	36
5	0	5	10	15	20	25	30	35	40	45
6	0	6	12	18	24	30	36	42	48	54
7	0	7	14	21	28	35	42	49	56	63
8	0	8	16	24	32	40	48	56	64	72
9	0	9	18	27	36	45	54	63	72	81

rows →

> TO FIND THE PRODUCT OF 3×4, MOVE YOUR FINGER TO THE COLUMN MARKED 3 AT THE TOP AND GO DOWN TO THE ROW MARKED 4. THE PRODUCT OF 3×4 IS 12.

What is the product of 7×9?
What is the product of 5×5?
What is the product of 8×2?

Remember!	Examples
If you multiply any number by 0, the product is 0.	$0 \times 4 = 0$ $0 \times 9 = 0$
If you multiply any number by 1, the product is that number.	$1 \times 7 = 7$ $1 \times 5 = 5$
If you change the order of the factors, the product is the same.	$6 \times 7 = 42$ $7 \times 6 = 42$

NOTE

When you read a vertical multiplication example, read up, saying the bottom factor first.

$$\begin{array}{r} 8 \\ \times\, 9 \\ \hline \end{array}$$

Say: 9 times 8 or nine eights.

MULTIPLYING 2-DIGIT NUMBERS

Using arrays helps you see how to multiply.

Multiply   14
          × 6

6 times

Draw an array on grid paper
that shows 14 squares 6 times.

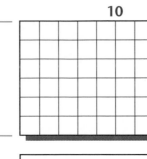

Use the array to multiply.

Multiply the ones: 14
                    × 6
                    ____
                     24

6×4

Multiply the tens: 14
                    × 6
                    ____
                     24
                     60

6×10

Add the tens and ones: 14
                        × 6
                        ____
                         24
                        +60
                        ____
                         84

$60 + 24$

YOU NEED TO KNOW YOUR TIMES TABLE BY HEART.

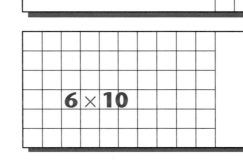

Here's a shorter way to multiply:

1. Multiply the ones.   2 $(6 \times 4 = 24$; 24 ones regroups to
   Regroup the 24 ones.   14   **2** tens and **4** ones)
                            × 6
                            ____
                              4

2. Multiply the tens.   2 $(6 \times 1$ ten = 6 tens)
   Add the regrouped   14   (6 tens + 2 tens = 8 tens)
   tens.   × 6
                            ____
                             84

Here's another way to make an array:

Multiply 12
× 8

You can use red checkers for the tens and black checkers for the ones. Arrange them in rows and columns like this. You need to make 8 rows of 12.

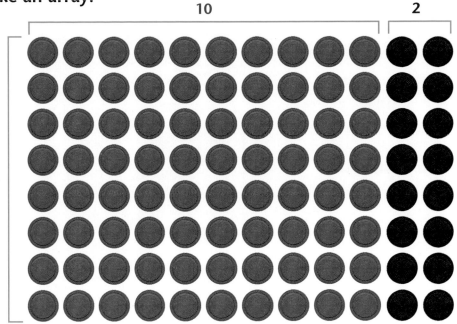

10   2

8 times

MULTIPLY THE ONES.

12
× 8
16

MULTIPLY THE TENS.

12
× 8
16
80

ADD.

12
× 8
16
+ 80
96

THIS IS THE FINAL PRODUCT.

Here's how to multiply 8 x 12 using the short method:

Multiply the ones.
  (8 × 2 = 16)
Regroup 16 ones.
  (16 = 1 ten and 6 ones)

1
12
× 8
6

Multiply the tens.
  (8 × 1 ten = 8 tens)
Add the regrouped tens.
  (8 tens + 1 ten = 9 tens)

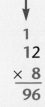

1
12
× 8
96

Great Graphs

HORIZONTAL GRAPHS

A **graph** is a way to show information.

One class voted on their favorite colors. Here's how they could show their votes in horizontal graphs:

THE WORD COLORS IS A COLUMN LABEL.

THIS IS THE TITLE OF THE PICTOGRAPH.

EACH 🙂 MEANS ONE CHILD'S VOTE.

Our Favorites

Colors	Votes
BLUE	🙂🙂🙂🙂
ORANGE	🙂🙂🙂🙂🙂🙂
GREEN	🙂🙂🙂
RED	🙂🙂🙂🙂🙂🙂🙂🙂🙂🙂🙂🙂

THE WORD VOTES IS A COLUMN LABEL, TOO.

THIS IS THE GRAPH TITLE.

THESE MARKS ARE CALLED TALLY MARKS.

Our Favorites

Colors	Votes
BLUE	IIII
ORANGE	⌧ I
GREEN	III
RED	⌧ ⌧ II

EACH VOTE GETS ONE TALLY MARK.

EACH GROUP OF FIVE TALLY MARKS LOOKS LIKE THIS ⌧.

Our Favorites

Colors	0	1	2	3	4	5	6	7	8	9	10	11	12	13	14	15
BLUE																
ORANGE																
GREEN																
RED																

Votes

YOU DON'T HAVE TO COUNT BOXES BECAUSE THEY ARE FILLED UP TO THE NUMBER OF VOTES.

EACH FILLED-IN BOX MEANS ONE VOTE.

ZERO MARKS THE BEGINNING OF THE NUMBERS.

VERTICAL GRAPHS

Another class counted items in a refrigerator. They listed what they found.

IN THE REFRIGERATOR

ITEMS	NUMBER
Cartons of Milk	2
Bottles of Juice	3
Eggs	12
Apples	6
Pears	8

Here's one way the children could make a vertical graph to show what they found:

EACH ROW IS LABELED WITH A NUMBER.

COUNT BY 2s TO READ EACH COLUMN.

In the Refrigerator

Division

HOW MANY
6s ARE IN 18?

DIVIDING WITHOUT REMAINDER

When you **divide**, you find out how many
of a number there are in another number.

THE NUMBER
YOU DIVIDE IS
THE DIVIDEND.

The sign ÷ means
divided by.

$$18 \div 6 = 3$$

THE ANSWER
IN DIVISION IS THE
QUOTIENT.

THE NUMBER
YOU DIVIDE BY IS
THE DIVISOR.

You can
also show
division
like this.

$$6\overline{)18}$$

Using Objects

You can model division with groups of objects.

For 24 ÷ 3, use 24 cubes.
Group the cubes by 3s.
Then count the groups.
There are 8 groups of 3 in 24.

$$24 \div 3 = 8$$

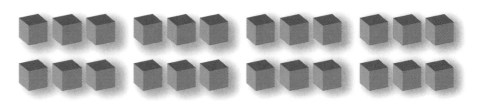

Using a Number Line

You can skip count back on a number line to show division.

For 24 ÷ 3, start at 24, the dividend. Skip count back by 3s to 0.

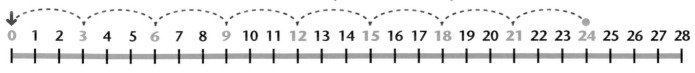

0 1 2 3 4 5 6 7 8 9 10 11 12 13 14 15 16 17 18 19 20 21 22 23 24 25 26 27 28

There are 8 jumps, so there are 8 groups of 3 in 24.   24 ÷ 3 = 8

DIVIDING WITH REMAINDER

When you divide a number, you sometimes have a **remainder**. Using counters helps you see how many groups you have and how many are left over.

Divide 27 by 8.

Use counters to find out how many groups of 8 there are in 27.

Use 27 counters. Group the counters into groups of 8.

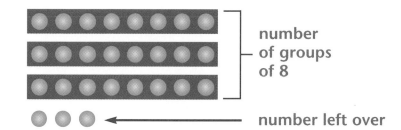

number of groups of 8

number left over

There are 3 groups of 8.
But there are 3 counters left over.
The number 3 is the remainder.

The equations may be written like this:

$27 \div 8 = 3$ R3 ← R means remainder.

$$8\overline{)27}^{\,3} \quad \text{R3}$$ ← R means remainder.

THE REMAINDER IS THE NUMBER LEFT OVER.

Use multiplication to help you divide.

Divide:

$$5\overline{)37}^{\,7}$$

THINK: WHAT NUMBER TIMES 5 IS CLOSE TO 37?
$7 \times 5 = 35$

Multiply:

$$5\overline{)37}^{\,7}$$
$$35 \leftarrow 7 \times 5 = 35$$

Subtract:

$$5\overline{)37}^{\,7} \quad \text{R2}$$
$$-35$$
$$\overline{2} \quad \text{remainder}$$

Remember!	Examples
Any number divided by 1 equals that number.	$7 \div 1 = 7$ $3 \div 1 = 3$
Any number (except 0) divided by itself equals 1.	$9 \div 9 = 1$ $4 \div 4 = 1$
Zero divided by any number (except 0) equals 0.	$0 \div 2 = 0$ $0 \div 5 = 0$

Take a Guess

PROBABILITY

Probability means how likely it is that an event will occur. You make predictions based on probability. You can do experiments to check your predictions.

If you spin the spinner 20 times, which color will it probably land on most?

1. **Predict** Look at the spinner. Think about which color the spinner will land on most and why. Since more sections are blue, the spinner will probably land on blue more often than any other color.

2. **Experiment** Spin the spinner 20 times. Keep a tally of the color it lands on each time.

3. **Record** Record the result of the experiment in a table like this:

Color	Tally Number	Total
White	III	3
Red	ℍℍ I	6
Blue	ℍℍ ℍℍ I	11

To use tally marks, make up-and-down lines as you count 1, 2, 3, and 4. Then when you count 5, make a slash through the first four lines.

4. **Check prediction** Compare the results of your experiment with your prediction. In this case you predicted the spinner would land on blue most often. It landed on blue 11 times, which is more than it landed on white or red. Your prediction was correct.

You can use what you learn from one experiment to make predictions for other experiments. An experiment you do for homework may be different from this one but your steps will be the same.

If you pick a crayon from a bag 15 times, and put it back after each pick, which color will you probably pick most often?

1. **Predict** Use what you learned from the spinner experiment to make this prediction. Since there are more black crayons than any other color, black will probably be picked most often.

2. **Experiment** Place the crayons in the bag. Pick out one crayon. Record the color and put the crayon back. Repeat 15 times.

3. **Record** Keep track of the colors you pick on a table like this:

Color	Tally Number	Total
Black	̶H̶H̶ I	6
Red	IIII	4
Blue	II	2
Yellow	III	3

4. **Check prediction** Your prediction was correct. Black was picked more often than any other color. Do the experiment 20 times to check further.

Other Experiments

- Put a variety of coins in a box. Pick and replace one coin at a time 25 times. Predict which coins will probably be picked most often and least often.
- Put a variety of colored socks in a drawer. Close your eyes and pick a sock and replace it 10 times. Predict which color will probably be picked most. Repeat the prediction and experiment by picking the sock only 5 times. Compare the results.

NOTE

These are experiments, so the results may not match predictions. Any careful recording is acceptable.

It's About Time

TELLING TIME

BOTH HANDS MOVE AROUND THE CLOCK, BUT THE HANDS MOVE AT DIFFERENT SPEEDS.

THE HOUR HAND MOVES ALL AROUND THE NUMBERS TWO TIMES EACH DAY. IT TAKES 24 HOURS TO MAKE A DAY.

THE MINUTE HAND TAKES 60 MINUTES TO GO AROUND ONCE. IT TAKES 1 HOUR TO GO AROUND THE CLOCK ONCE.

The long hand is the minute hand.

The short hand is the hour hand.

EACH TICK LINE MARKS 1 MINUTE. IT TAKES THE MINUTE HAND 1 MINUTE TO GO FROM TICK TO TICK. IT TAKES 5 MINUTES TO GO FROM NUMBER TO NUMBER.

THE HOUR HAND TAKES 60 MINUTES TO MOVE FROM ONE NUMBER TO THE NEXT. IT TAKES 1 HOUR TO GO FROM 8 TO 9.

I COUNT THE TICKS BY 5s, IT'S FASTER: 5, 10, 15, 20, 25, 30!

These clocks show how the hour and minute hands move as time passes.

It is four o'clock.
4:00

The minute hand points to the 12, and the hour hand points directly to the 4.

Now it is thirty minutes after four.
4:30

You can see that the minute hand has moved 30 minutes, halfway around the clock. The hour hand has moved halfway from the 4 to the 5.

ANALOG AND DIGITAL CLOCKS

Here the hour hand is just past the 1. The minute hand points to 3.

1. Say the hour. **One**.
2. Count the ticks from the 12 to the 3 and say the minutes. **Fifteen**.

The time is one-fifteen, or **1:15**.
On the digital clock, it says **1:15**.

On this clock, the hour hand points halfway between 3 and 4. The minute hand points to 7.

1. Say the hour just passed. **Three**.
2. Count the ticks from the 12 to the 7 and say the minutes. **Thirty-five**.

The time is three thirty-five, or **3:35**.
On the digital clock, it says **3:35**.

1:15 on a digital clock

3:35 on a digital clock

1:15 on an analog clock

3:35 on an analog clock

You can write or say what time it is in more than one way.

5:15

five-fifteen
fifteen minutes past five
quarter past five

10:45

ten forty-five
forty-five minutes past ten
quarter to eleven
fifteen minutes to eleven

3:55

three fifty-five
five minutes to four

6:40

six-forty
forty minutes past six
twenty minutes to seven

8:30

eight-thirty
thirty minutes past eight
half past eight
thirty minutes to nine

12:00

twelve o'clock
noon (daytime)
midnight (nighttime)

Going to Great Lengths

CUSTOMARY UNITS OF LENGTH

Length is the distance from one point to another.

Customary units of length are inch, foot, yard, and mile.
Customary units are also called American Standard units.

Customary units of length are related in the following way:

12 inches = 1 foot
36 inches = 1 yard
3 feet = 1 yard
5,280 feet = 1 mile
1,760 yards = 1 mile

You can also measure the length of any object using **nonstandard** units.

 This line measures:

 6 connecting cubes long

 2 paper clips long

 3 pennies long

Because **nonstandard** units give a different measurement depending on what unit is used, **standard** units are most often used to measure length.

Customary Units of Length	Things that are about that length
1 inch (in)	a paper clip knuckle to the tip of the thumb
1 foot (ft)	a celery stalk a man's sneaker
1 yard (yd)	a baseball bat a bookshelf

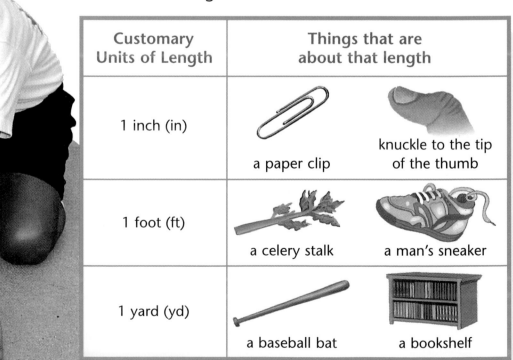

METRIC UNITS OF LENGTH

Metric units are used in most countries of the world. **Metric units of length** are centimeter, decimeter, meter, and kilometer. Metric units are based on multiples of ten.

Metric units of length are related in the following way:

10 centimeters = 1 decimeter
100 centimeters = 1 meter
10 decimeters = 1 meter
1,000 meters = 1 kilometer

Metric Units of Length	Things that are about that length	
1 centimeter (cm)	the width of a fingernail	the width of a paper clip
1 decimeter (dm)	a crayon	a piece of chalk
1 meter (m)	the width of a window	the distance from the top of a table to the floor

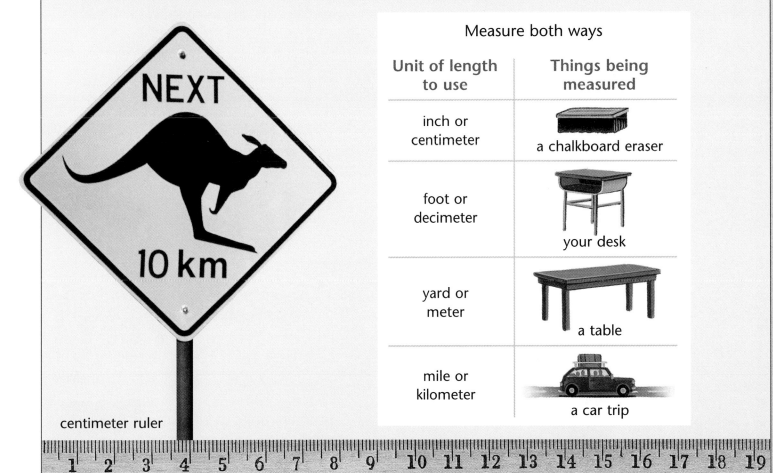

Measure both ways

Unit of length to use	Things being measured
inch or centimeter	a chalkboard eraser
foot or decimeter	your desk
yard or meter	a table
mile or kilometer	a car trip

NEXT 10 km

centimeter ruler

1 2 3 4 5 6 7 8 9 10 11 12 13 14 15 16 17 18 19

Heavy Thinking

CUSTOMARY UNITS OF WEIGHT

Weight tells how heavy an object is. Commonly used measurements of weight are ounce, pound, ton, gram, and kilogram.

Customary units of weight are used in the United States to tell how much an object weighs.

Here are the most commonly used customary units of weight and examples of objects that weigh about that amount:

Customary Units of Weight	Things that weigh about that amount	
1 ounce (oz)	a strawberry	a ping-pong ball
1 pound (lb)	a loaf of bread	a basketball
1 ton (ton)	a car	a young elephant

Customary units of weight are related in the following way:

1 pound = 16 ounces
1 ton = 2,000 pounds

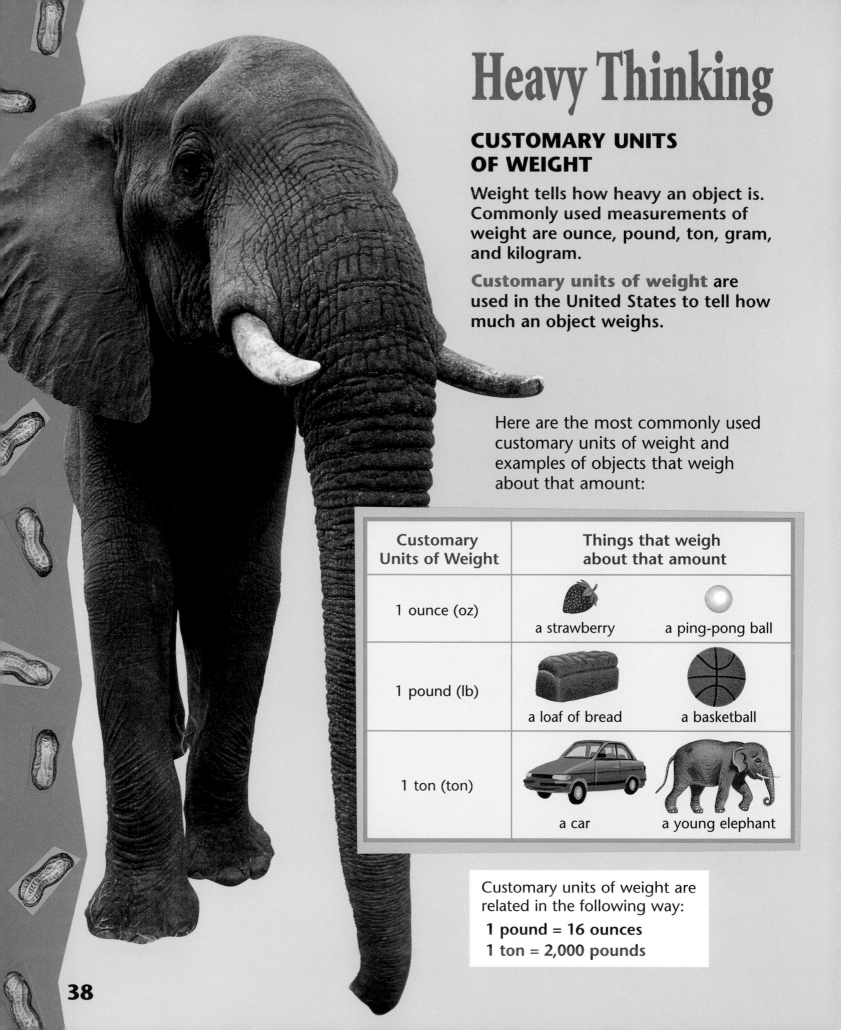

METRIC UNITS OF WEIGHT

Metric units of weight are used in most countries of the world. Metric units are based on multiples of ten.

Here are examples of standard units of weight in the metric system:

Metric Units of Weight	Things that weigh about that amount
1 gram (g)	a large paper clip a peanut
1 kilogram (kg)	a dictionary a kitten

Metric units of weight are related in the following way:

1 kilogram = 1,000 grams

Understanding how much each unit of weight is will help you decide on the correct unit of measurement to use to measure the weight of different objects. Here are some examples:

Unit of weight to use	Things being weighed
gram or ounce	a box of pencils
kilogram or pound	a dog
ton	a truck

Hold It Right There!

CUSTOMARY UNITS OF CAPACITY

Capacity is the amount of liquid a container can hold.

Customary units of capacity, used in the United States, are cup, pint, quart, and gallon.

Customary Units of Capacity	Containers that hold about that amount	
1 cup (c)	a cup	a juice box
1 pint (pt)	a cream container	a soda-pop can
1 quart (qt)	a milk container	a motor oil can
1 gallon (gal)	a jug	a fish bowl

This table shows how customary units of capacity are related.

Equivalent Amounts			
gallon	quart	pint	cup
1 =	4 =	8 =	16
	1 =	2 =	4
		1 =	2

NOTE

The smallest customary unit of capacity is a fluid **ounce**. There are 8 ounces in a cup, 16 ounces in a pint, 32 ounces in a quart, and 128 ounces in a gallon.

METRIC UNITS OF CAPACITY

You can also measure capacity using metric units of measurement. **Metric units of capacity are milliliter and liter.** Metric units are based on multiples of ten.

Metric units of capacity are related in the following way:

1 liter = 1,000 milliliters

Here are examples of metric units of capacity and examples of containers that hold each amount:

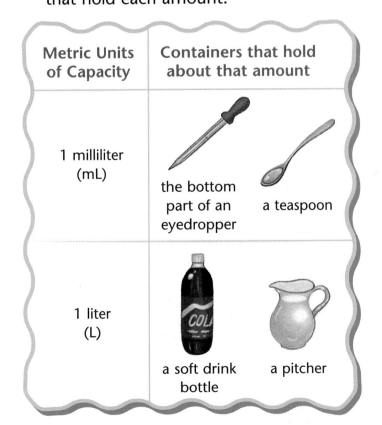

Metric Units of Capacity	Containers that hold about that amount
1 milliliter (mL)	the bottom part of an eyedropper · a teaspoon
1 liter (L)	a soft drink bottle · a pitcher

Understanding how much each unit of capacity is will help you decide on the correct unit of measurement to use to measure different amounts. Here are some examples:

Unit of capacity to use	Capacity being measured
ounce or cup or milliliter	milk in a glass
pint or milliliter	container of cream
quart or liter	water in a pail
gallon or liter	water in a pool

Inside and Around

AREA

Area is the number of square units it takes to cover the surface of a figure.

To measure the area of these figures, count the total number of square units in each rectangle.

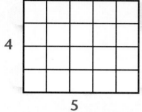

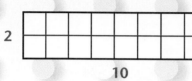

20 square units   **20 square units**

To figure the area without counting each unit, multiply the number of length units by the number of width units.

$5 \times 4 = 20$
units   units   square units

$10 \times 2 = 20$
units   units   square units

Both of these figures have the same area: 20 square units.

Comparing Area

You can use dotted paper to draw figures that look different but have the same area.

Here are 2 figures that each have an area of 10 square units:

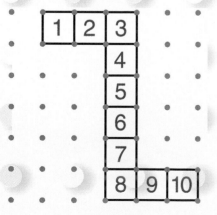

NOTE

Square units are used to measure area. The units may be:

square inches
square feet
square yards
square centimeters
square decimeters
square meters
square miles
square kilometers

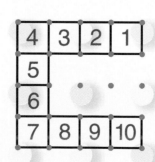

WHAT IS THE AREA OF THE RED PART OF THIS FIGURE?

THE AREA OF THE RED PART IS 2 SQUARE UNITS—ONE WHOLE SQUARE AND TWO HALVES.

PERIMETER

Perimeter is the number of units around a figure.

EACH ▬ IS AN INCH. WHAT IS THE PERIMETER OF THIS PICTURE?

To measure the perimeter of these figures, count the units around each rectangle.

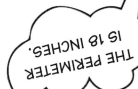

THE PERIMETER IS 18 INCHES.

Each ▬ is a centimeter.

To figure perimeter, without counting, add the two lengths and the two widths.

Each ▬ is a centimeter.

4 + 4 + 3 + 3 = 14

5 + 5 + 2 + 2 = 14

The perimeter is 14 centimeters.
The area is 12 square centimeters.

The perimeter is 14 centimeters.
The area is 10 square centimeters.

What's My Line?

LINES AND ANGLES

This is a **point**: •

A **line** is a set of points joined to each other in a straight path. This is a line:

A line goes on forever and ever.
A line segment has a beginning and an end.

Here is a **line segment**: ⎯⎯⎯⎯⎯⎯⎯
A line segment is the straight path between two points.

When two line segments share one end point, they might look like this.

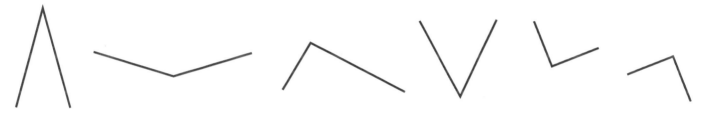

The space from line segment to line segment is an **angle**.

angle   angle

These triangle **shapes** are made with 3 line segments.
They have 3 sides and 3 angles.

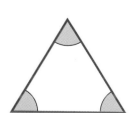 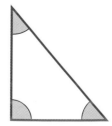 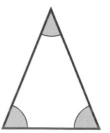

You can make many kinds of shapes on a geoboard.

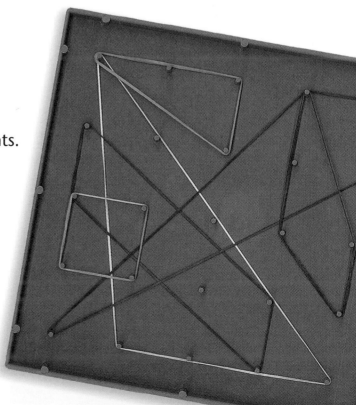

44

THREE KINDS OF ANGLES

This is a **right angle**.

This is an **acute angle**.
It is smaller than a right angle.

This is an **obtuse angle**.
It is bigger than a right angle.

What were the function machine's orders?

| When two lines go in, make the lines into a right angle. | When two lines go in, make the lines into an acute angle. | When two lines go in, make the lines into an obtuse angle. |

Shape Up!

PLANE SHAPES

A **plane shape** is a flat shape.
A plane shape has two dimensions.

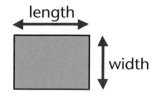

length

width

Polygons

A **polygon** is a plane shape made by joining 3 or more line segments.

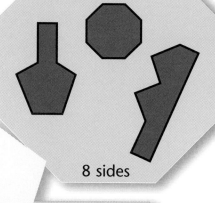

OCTAGONS

8 sides

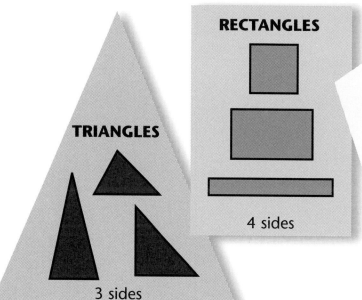

RECTANGLES

4 sides

TRIANGLES

3 sides

PENTAGONS

5 sides

HEXAGONS

6 sides

Closed Curve Shapes

A **closed curve shape** is a plane shape made with curved lines.

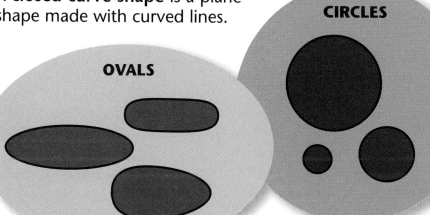

OVALS

CIRCLES

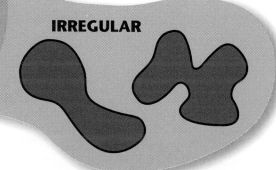

IRREGULAR

NOTE

A **square** is a rectangle with four equal sides.

46

SOLID SHAPES

A solid shape is not flat.

A solid figure has three dimensions.

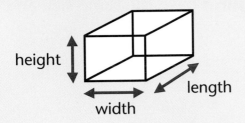

height

width

length

Words that describe parts of a solid are:

face

corner

edge

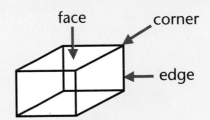

curved surface

face

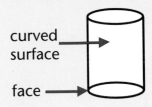

RECTANGULAR PRISM
6 faces
Each face is a rectangle.

CYLINDER
2 faces
Each face is a circle.

CONE
1 face
One face is a circle.

PYRAMID
5 faces
Four faces are triangles.
One face is a square.

SPHERE
no faces

NOTE

A **cube** is a rectangular prism. Each face is a square.

Here, There, Everywhere				
rectangular prisms	cylinders	cones	pyramids	spheres
cereal boxes	cans of food	party hats	Egyptian pyramids	baseballs
buildings	oatmeal containers		roofs of square-shaped houses	globes of the world
refrigerators	new pencils			clowns' noses
number cubes	light poles	ice cream cones	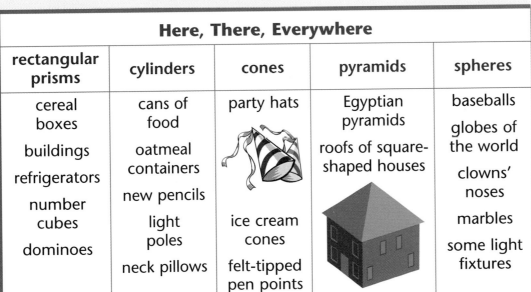	marbles
dominoes	neck pillows	felt-tipped pen points		some light fixtures

Figure It Out

CONGRUENT FIGURES

Congruent figures have the same size and shape.

To find if the black rectangle is congruent to rectangles A, B, or C, you can:

1. Trace the rectangle.

2. Match your copy of the rectangle with each figure.

 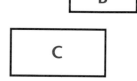

Only Figure C is congruent to the black rectangle. A is the wrong shape and B is the wrong size.

You can draw congruent figures using dotted grid paper. To draw a figure congruent to each red figure on the left, draw lines that connect the same number of dots in the same shape.

Congruent figures can be in different positions, but must be the same size and shape as the original.

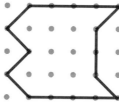   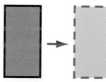

Slide   Flip   Turn

NOTE

Figures that are the same shape but not the same size are called **similar**.

48

SYMMETRY

A line of **symmetry** divides a figure into two matching parts. Figures that have one or more lines of symmetry are **symmetrical**.

Here is a shape with a line of symmetry. The two sides match exactly.

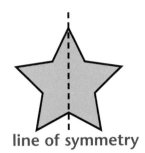

line of symmetry

Here is a shape that does not have a line of symmetry. You can not draw a line through this shape to show two matching parts.

no line of symmetry

You can use dotted grid paper to draw symmetrical designs.

line of symmetry

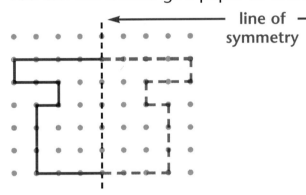

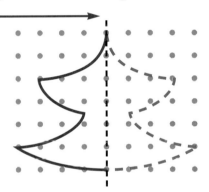

Some shapes have only one line of symmetry.

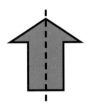 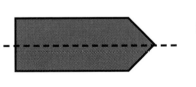

Some shapes have more than one line of symmetry.

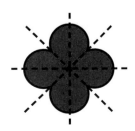 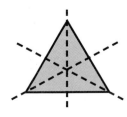 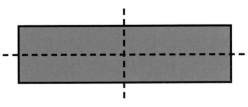

NOTE

Circles are special symmetrical shapes. They have an unlimited number of lines of symmetry. Any line that passes through the center of a circle is a line of symmetry.

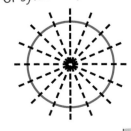

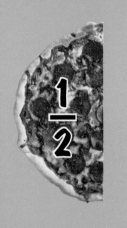

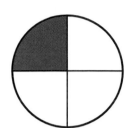

Name That Part

FRACTIONS OF A WHOLE

A **fraction** is a number that describes the parts of a whole.
A fraction is made up of a **numerator** and **denominator**.

What fraction describes the
shaded part of the whole circle?

1 ← numerator: number of shaded parts

$\overline{4}$ ← denominator: total number of equal parts

Here are fraction strips that show different fractions:

Count the total number of parts in the strip.
That number is the denominator.

Count the number of shaded parts in the strip.
That number is the numerator.

$\dfrac{2}{3}$ shaded parts total parts

$\dfrac{5}{6}$ shaded parts total parts

$\dfrac{3}{4}$ shaded parts total parts

You can use fraction strips to compare fractions:

These fraction strips show that $\dfrac{1}{3}$ is greater than $\dfrac{1}{4}$.

$\dfrac{1}{3}$

$\dfrac{1}{4}$

$\dfrac{1}{3} > \dfrac{1}{4}$

These fraction strips show that the fraction $\dfrac{3}{6}$ is equal to the fraction $\dfrac{1}{2}$.

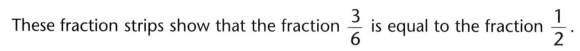

$\dfrac{3}{6}$

$\dfrac{1}{2}$

Fractions that represent equal amounts
are called **equivalent fractions**.

$\dfrac{3}{6}$ and $\dfrac{1}{2}$ are equivalent fractions. $\dfrac{3}{6} = \dfrac{1}{2}$

FRACTIONS OF A SET

A fraction can be used to describe a part of a set.

Here is a set of 4 cars. How many are black?
How many are red?

3 out of a total of 4 cars are black: $\frac{3}{4}$ are black.

1 out of a total of 4 cars is red: $\frac{1}{4}$ is red.

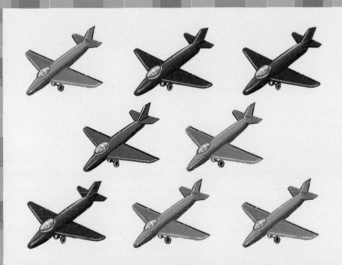

Here is a set of 8 planes.
How many are red? blue? green?

3 of the 8 planes are red: $\frac{3}{8}$ are red.

1 of the 8 planes is blue: $\frac{1}{8}$ is blue.

4 of the 8 planes are green: $\frac{4}{8}$ are green.

Here is a set of model boats.
I low many are there altogether?
How many are standing up?
How many are tipped over?

5 out of 6 boats are up: $\frac{5}{6}$ are up.

1 out of 6 boats is tipped: $\frac{1}{6}$ is tipped.

Joining the Parts

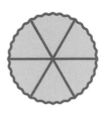

ADDING FRACTIONS
with like denominators

To **add fractions** with like denominators, add the numerators and keep the same denominator.

$$\frac{1}{6} + \frac{2}{6} = \begin{array}{l} \longrightarrow \text{ add the numerators} \longrightarrow \frac{3}{6} \\ \longrightarrow \text{ keep the same denominator} \longrightarrow \frac{3}{6} \end{array}$$

Here's how to use fraction strips to add fractions with like denominators:

Add: $\frac{3}{8} + \frac{2}{8}$

1. Show a fraction strip for $\frac{3}{8}$.

2. Put a fraction strip for $\frac{2}{8}$ next to the $\frac{3}{8}$.

3. Count the total number of shaded parts.

   There are $\frac{5}{8}$ in all: $\frac{3}{8} + \frac{2}{8} = \frac{5}{8}$

Here's another way to use fraction strips:

Add: $\frac{1}{5} + \frac{3}{5}$

1. Take a fifths fraction strip.

2. Shade $\frac{1}{5}$ in one color.

3. Shade $\frac{3}{5}$ in another color.

4. Count the shaded fifths: $\frac{1}{5} + \frac{3}{5} = \frac{4}{5}$

52

Solve a Problem by Adding Fractions

Suppose you and a friend make a pizza with 8 equal slices, and you each put on your favorite topping. If you put mushrooms on 2 slices and your friend puts peppers on 3 slices, how much of the pizza would have toppings?

$$\frac{2}{8} + \frac{3}{8} = ?$$

Count $\frac{2}{8}$. Count on $\frac{3}{8}$ more.

$$\frac{2}{8} + \frac{3}{8} = \frac{5}{8}$$

Five-eighths of the pizza would have toppings.

You can use drawings to help when you add fractions.

Add: $\frac{1}{6} + \frac{3}{6}$

1. Draw 6 circles to show the total number of parts (the denominator).

2. Shade 1 circle to show $\frac{1}{6}$.

   Shade 3 more circles to show $\frac{3}{6}$.

3. Count the total number of shaded circles: $\frac{1}{6} + \frac{3}{6} = \frac{4}{6}$

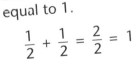

NOTE

When the numerator and the denominator are the same, the fraction is equal to 1.

$$\frac{1}{2} + \frac{1}{2} = \frac{2}{2} = 1$$

$\frac{2}{2}$ is the same as 1

$$\frac{1}{7} + \frac{6}{7} = \frac{7}{7} = 1$$

$\frac{7}{7}$ is the same as 1

What Part Is Left?

SUBTRACTING FRACTIONS
with like denominators

To **subtract fractions** with like denominators, subtract the numerators and keep the same denominator.

$$\frac{3}{4} - \frac{2}{4} = \quad \longrightarrow \text{ subtract the numerators } \longrightarrow \frac{1}{4}$$
$$\longrightarrow \text{ keep the same denominator } \longrightarrow$$

Here's how to use fraction strips to subtract fractions with like denominators:

Subtract: $\frac{7}{8} - \frac{2}{8}$

1. Show a fraction strip for $\frac{7}{8}$.

2. Put a fraction strip for $\frac{2}{8}$ below the first fraction strip.

3. Count the difference in the number of shaded parts.

   There is a difference of $\frac{5}{8}$: $\frac{7}{8} - \frac{2}{8} = \frac{5}{8}$

Here's another way to use fraction strips:

Subtract: $\frac{5}{6} - \frac{2}{6}$

1. Show a sixths fraction strip.

2. Shade $\frac{5}{6}$ in one color.

3. Cross out or cover $\frac{2}{6}$ of the shaded parts.

4. Count the shaded sixths that are left.

   There are $\frac{3}{6}$ left: $\frac{5}{6} - \frac{2}{6} = \frac{3}{6}$

Solve a Problem by Subtracting Fractions

Suppose you cut a cake into 6 equal pieces and ate $\frac{1}{6}$ of the cake. You see that $\frac{5}{6}$ of the cake is left. If you give a friend another $\frac{1}{6}$, how much cake would be left?

$$\frac{5}{6} - \frac{1}{6} = ?$$

Count $\frac{5}{6}$. Count back $\frac{1}{6}$.

$$\frac{5}{6} - \frac{1}{6} = \frac{4}{6}$$

There would be $\frac{4}{6}$ of the cake left.

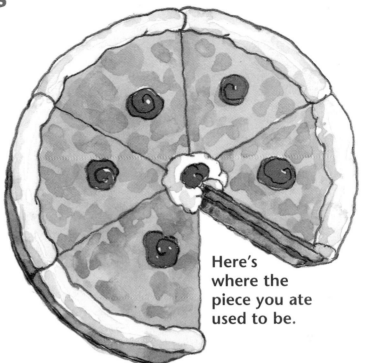

Here's where the piece you ate used to be.

You can use drawings to help when you subtract fractions.

Subtract: $\frac{5}{8} - \frac{3}{8}$

1. Draw 8 circles to show the total number of parts (the denominator).

2. Shade 5 circles to show $\frac{5}{8}$.

3. Cross out 3 shaded circles to show you are taking away $\frac{3}{8}$ from the $\frac{5}{8}$.

4. Count the total number of shaded circles left. There are $\frac{2}{8}$ left: $\frac{5}{8} - \frac{3}{8} = \frac{2}{8}$

Talking About Decimals

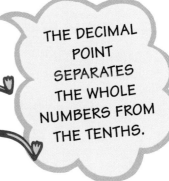

COMPARING TENTHS

A **decimal number** is another way of expressing a fraction.

This square is divided into ten equal parts.

   One of the ten parts is green.

   One tenth of the square is green. You can write one tenth as a fraction.

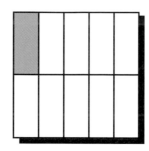

$\dfrac{1}{10}$ ← **The 1 means the 1 green part.**

← **The 10 means the whole was divided into 10 equal parts.**

Or, you can write $\dfrac{1}{10}$ as a decimal number like this: 0.1

Read the fraction and the decimal number for each green part in these shapes.

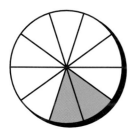

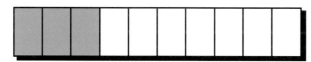

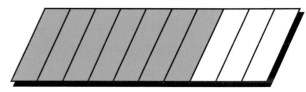

$\dfrac{2}{10}$ or 0.2

$\dfrac{3}{10}$ or 0.3

$\dfrac{7}{10}$ or 0.7

Place Value

Here is the number fifty-seven and one tenth: 57.1

Here is 57.1 in a place-value chart.

tens	ones	tenths
5	7 •	1

Here are some more decimal numbers:

tens	ones	tenths
	7 •	1
	0 •	4
	1 •	9
1	3 •	5
2	0 •	6

seven and one tenth

four tenths

one and nine tenths

thirteen and five tenths

twenty and six tenths

THE DECIMAL POINT SEPARATES THE WHOLE NUMBERS FROM THE TENTHS.

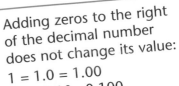

NOTE

Adding zeros to the right of the decimal number does not change its value:

1 = 1.0 = 1.00
0.1 = 0.10 = 0.100
3.2 = 3.20 = 3.200

Look at each square. See which part is shaded.

0.4 (four tenths)   **0.9** (nine tenths)

THIS SYMBOL > MEANS IS GREATER THAN. THIS ONE < MEANS IS LESS THAN.

Which is less?
The models show that 0.4 < 0.9, or four tenths is less than nine tenths.

A square with all ten parts shaded represents one whole.

1.2 (one and two tenths)   **2.7** (two and seven tenths)

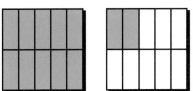   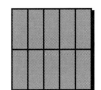

Which is greater?
The models show that 2.7 > 1.2, or two and seven tenths is greater than one and two tenths.

Using Money to Compare Decimals

You can use dimes to model decimals because one dime is one tenth of a dollar.

0.6 or **$.60**   **0.4** or **$.40**

Which is greater?
The money shows that 0.6 > 0.4, or six tenths is greater than four tenths.

Comparing Decimal Numbers

Compare the whole numbers, then compare the tenths.

3.5 < 3.8	42.5 < 42.7
5.8 > 5.2	15.8 > 15.1
6.4 > 6.0	80.1 < 80.5

If one whole number is greater than the other, you do not have to compare the tenths.

6.7 > 3.8	4.9 < 7.8
3.8 > 1.5	8.3 < 10.6

Problem-Solving Strategies

USE OBJECTS

Here's an example of how to use objects to solve word problems:

Read the problem: There are 4 people on a bus. At the first stop, 3 of the people get off. At the next stop, 5 people get on. How many people are now on the bus?

What is the information?
4 people are on the bus
3 people get off
5 people get on

What is the question?
How many people are now on the bus?

Use objects to show what happened:

First, show 4 unit blocks to stand for the people on the bus.

Then, take away 3 blocks to stand for the people who get off at the first stop.

Add 5 blocks to stand for the people who get on at the next stop.

Choose the operations: Will you add, subtract, multiply, or divide?
Subtract to find how many people were left after 3 people got off.
Add to find how many people were in the bus after 5 got on.

Do the operations and answer the question:
First,   4 − 3 = 1
Then,   1 + 5 = 6   **Answer:** There are 6 people now on the bus.

Here's another example:

You have 12 pennies. You want to give an equal number to 3 friends. How many pennies will you give each friend?

Use 12 pennies and 3 boxes. Put 1 penny in each box until all the pennies are in boxes. How many pennies will each friend get?

Answer: Each friend will get 4 pennies.

GUESS AND CHECK

Here's an example of how to use guess and check to solve a homework word problem:

Read the problem: The sum of Spot's and Pal's ages is 12. Pal is 2 years younger than Spot. How old is each dog?

What is the information?

Spot's age + Pal's age = 12

Spot's age – Pal's age = 2

What is the question?

How old is each dog?

Guess and check: Guess reasonable answers and then check to see if they make sense with the information you have.

▶ **Guess:** Try any two numbers that add up to 12: Try 8 and 4.

▶ **Check:** If Spot is 8 and Pal is 4, is Pal 2 years younger than Spot? 8 – 4 = 4. No.

Guess again: Since the difference between 8 and 4 is too great, try two other numbers that are closer to each other and still have a sum of 12.

▶ **Guess:** Try 7 and 5.

▶ **Check:** If Spot is 7 and Pal is 5, is Pal 2 years younger than Spot? 7 – 5 = 2. Yes.

Answer the question: **Answer:** Spot is 7 and Pal is 5.

Here's another example:

You want to spend exactly $10.

Which two of these things can you buy?

$3 pen $8 book $7 calculator $4 stapler

▶ **Guess:** Try any two items. Try a book and pen.

▶ **Check:** Does the total equal $10? $8 + $3 = $11. No.

Guess again: Since the total was too high, try a lower number.

▶ **Guess:** Try a calculator and pen.

▶ **Check:** Does the total cost equal $10? $7 + $3 = $10. Yes.

Answer: You can buy a pen and a calculator.

DRAW A PICTURE

This example shows how to draw a picture of the information given in a word problem, and how to use it to solve the problem.

> **Read the problem:** Pat has three boxes. Two boxes have 1 car each. The third box has 3 cars. How many cars does Pat have in all?

What is the information?

    Pat has three boxes.

    Two boxes have 1 car each.

    The third box has 3 cars.

What is the question?

    How many cars does Pat have in all?

Draw a picture:

    First draw three empty boxes, then draw the cars.

      1 car   **1 car**   **3 cars**

Choose the operation: Will you add, subtract, multiply, or divide?

    Add the cars in each box to find the total number of cars.

Do the operation and answer the question:

    1 + 1 + 3 = 5   **Answer:** Pat has 5 cars in all.

Here's another example:

There are 12 children in the room. Only 5 of them are girls. How many are boys? Use a picture.

Label 5 of the pictures with a <u>G</u> for girls. Count the rest to find the number of boys.

Answer: There are 7 boys.

CHOOSE THE INFORMATION YOU NEED

Here's an example of how to choose the information you need to solve a word problem:

> **Read the problem:**
> There are 12 pigeons and 6 sparrows on a roof. Then 4 of the pigeons fly away. How many pigeons are left on the roof?

What is the question?

How many pigeons are left on the roof?

Choose the information you need to answer the question:

Since the question is only about pigeons, the information about the pigeons is what you need.

There are 12 pigeons.

~~There are 6 sparrows.~~

Then 4 of the pigeons fly away.

Choose the operation: Will you add, subtract, multiply, or divide?

To find out how many are left, you subtract.

Do the operation and answer the question:

12 – 4 = 8   Answer: There are 8 pigeons left on the roof.

Here's another example:

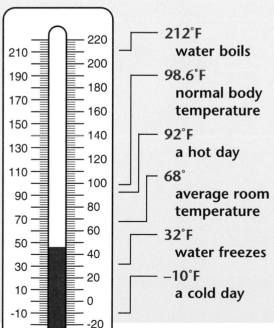

212°F
water boils

98.6°F
normal body
temperature

92°F
a hot day

68°
average room
temperature

32°F
water freezes

–10°F
a cold day

This thermometer shows Fahrenheit temperatures.

What is the difference between average room temperature and the temperature at which water freezes?

Look at the diagram to find out the average room temperature (68°) and at what temperature water freezes (32°). Then subtract to find the difference.

Answer: 68° – 32° = 36°
The difference is 36°.

MAKE A LIST

Here's an example of how to make a list to solve word problems when you do your homework:

Read the problem: There are 3 boys in line in this order: Alex, Harry, Carlos. If the boys change places, how many different ways can they stand in line?

What is the information?
3 boys are in line.
The boys change places.

What is the question?
How many different ways can the boys stand in line?

Make a list to show all the possible combinations:

Alex
Harry
Carlos

Alex
Carlos
Harry

Harry
Alex
Carlos

Harry
Carlos
Alex

Carlos
Alex
Harry

Carlos
Harry
Alex

Solve the problem and answer the question:
Count the number of different ways listed.
Answer: The boys can stand in 6 different ways.

Here's another example:
How many different ways can you make 35 cents, using at least 1 quarter? Make a list.   **Answer: There are 4 ways.**

1 quarter and 1 dime   1 quarter and 2 nickels
1 quarter, 1 nickel, and 5 pennies   1 quarter and 10 pennies

LOOK FOR A PATTERN

Here's an example of how to look for a pattern and use it to solve a homework word problem:

> **Read the problem:**
> Bob is building with cubes. If he follows this pattern, how many cubes would the completed design have?

Row 1
Row 2
Row 3
Row 4
Row 5
Row 6

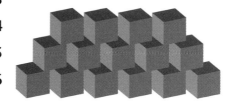

What is the information?

There are 6 cubes in Row 6.

There are 5 cubes in Row 5.

There are 4 cubes in Row 4.

What is the question?

How many cubes would the completed design have?

Look for a pattern:

In this pattern, the number of cubes matches the number of the row. If you continue this pattern, Row 3 would have 3 cubes, Row 2 would have 2 cubes, and Row 1 would have 1 cube.

Choose the operation: Will you add, subtract, multiply, or divide?

Continue the pattern. Then add the numbers for each row to find out how many cubes in all would complete the design.

Do the operation. Answer the question: $6 + 5 + 4 + 3 + 2 + 1 = 21$

Answer: The completed design would have 21 cubes.

Here's another example:

You save $3 in Week 1, $6 in Week 2, and $12 in Week 3. If you continue to save money in this pattern, how much would you save in Week 5? Make a table and look for a pattern:

In this pattern, each week the amount saved is twice the amount of the week before.

Savings					
Week	1	2	3	4	5
Amount	$3	$6	$12	?	?

Multiply to find how much would be saved in Week 4: $2 \times \$12 = \$24$.
Then multiply to find how much would be saved in Week 5:
$2 \times \$24 = \$48$.   **Answer:** You would save $48 dollars in Week 5.

Index